Passages

By Jacqueline Robinson

Published by Jewelmark Press 2011

A CIP record for this book is available from
the British Library

ISBN 978-0-9562727-1-3

Cover design by Chris Calderon

Dedicated with love to

Asore, Jewel

and Sakina

Contents

Passages

Key Features

As soon as I glimpse your
Six foot ebony frame
An unrivalled desire wells up within me
I feel a compulsion to draw near to you
And run my fingers up and down
Your smooth body
So, responsive to my touch
Immediately I become suspended
In time and space
Caught up in a rhapsody of music
Only I can hear

When I peruse
Your undulating feminine curves
I am translated to a place where
Pleasure and pride are intermingled
Forming a heady cocktail driving me to the
Point of drunken excitement
You are so beautiful

I vow to become more skilled as your lover
So I can bring out the very best in you
Your full bodied tones
Massage my mind
Causing my stresses and cares to disappear

My friends don't understand our relationship
Neither do they appreciate you
As much as I do
Some have said they would not even
Give you a second glance
They don't even understand
Why we're together
But they can't influence my love for you
To me baby, you'll always be grand

Precipitation

As I stand in this torrent of rain
I have the vain hope that
The constant saturation
Will dampen the fury I feel towards you
As each drop smacks me
Around my head and beats my body
I remember the pain you caused
When you said 'I think we should call it a day'
Withdrawing from
What I thought was a forever love
You were proud to have me
As your trophy girl
'Foxy Lady' you called me
Envy of your friends
Now I hear you are calling me 'A Vixen'
Who is manipulating and deceiving
With a beauty that stops at the skin
And never as deep as the soul
Dumped – you have consigned me
To the rubbish heap of your life
Tossed onto the pile of the forgotten

Rage controls my thoughts and actions
I've dreamed of burning down
Your house or car

I've even tried to imagine
How it would feel
To twist a knife in your gut
Self-preservation is my only restraint

I'm confused, did I really love you?
Maybe I was in love with
The constant gifts, affection
And high life you brought along with you
I don't know
So infatuated
I didn't see the end coming

Oh cold harsh rain
Flush him from the door of my heart
Into the gutter where he belongs

Despair

I'm stuck in this dungeon
Of flabby flesh
No way out
Scared stiff
My only friend food
Is really my enemy
Killing me
So slowly

Viagra Victim

On and on
When will this end?
Pleasure, got up and left the room
Ages ago
Leaving me on my own
Suffering in silence
I'm so bored
Actually wishing
I was doing something else
Once again
It's all about you

Youthful Sight

Looking at the world with your youthful eyes
You readily believe in the purity
Of love and happiness
Appalled and rejecting the thought that
Love can ever hurt or make you sad
Unable to comprehend that
Something so rich
Can spring up, grow and die
Leaving nothing but the seed of pain behind
To be nurtured by the rain of bitterness
And the burning sun of emptiness

You have a liberty
Which allows you to speak your mind
Without the restraint of trepidation or fear
You see life as an expression of freedom
Unhampered by caution
Or the constant assessment of consequences
Through your spring like vision
Every opportunity is there to be maximised
A chance to make fleeting friendships
Experience laughter and have fun

Enjoy this time my child
Because the passage of time
Growth and maturity
Will change your perspective
Incidents will gnaw away your innocence
Leaving you with nothing but distorted sight

Different

I never knew I was different until
Mum told me that I was not related
To anyone in my family
No shared blood, no common genes
Her words flattened my blissful world
Like a fist on plasticine
All structure completely destroyed

I began to realise the jokes
I had often laughed at and joined in with
Were actually spiteful remarks in disguise
About me, my size
The colour of my skin
The texture of my hair
Even the colour of my eyes

I notice I never seem to qualify for the finest
Like the 'real' children
I am always second best
Doing the dirtiest and longest chores
Whilst the others play
Never getting the smartest clothes
Or the new toys
Not even a book to call my own

In my secret place
Hidden from the world
I cannot count the many tears
Born out of frustration and anger
That have rolled down my face
Making my cheeks sore
I 've spent hours trying to fathom
Why I am rejected
Accepted by none

Is it's my fault?
What did I do wrong?
Every day I plan to run away
Wanting to escape my daily torture of
Watching affection being lavished
On the other kids
My turn never quite arriving
Hope repeatedly
Crushed by disappointment
I just want to be hugged
Told that I am loved too
But I only get distant smiles

I am an isolated 12 year old
With a broken heart
That will never be fixed

Don't' Knock the Gas Man

I'm telling you girlfriend
The Gas Man is coming TODAY!
I can't wait

As soon as I got the gas appointment
I sorted out the others
Hair nails, facial
I selected my outfit
With such precision and attention to detail
I'm dressing to entice
Seduction in mind
The Gas Man is coming TODAY

Who says you have to get out there
To find an attractive man?
He's coming right into my home
Let me tell you
This Gas Man
Can inspect my pipe any time
He's so, so, so, fine
You see he's been before
Tall, lean, and strong
I caught myself drooling
At his taught frame the last time
Oh the Gas Man is coming TODAY

I can't wait

I open the door
Playing it cool
He and his mate enter
With trivial conversation
I calmly offer tea
Trying to hide the fact that
My heart is racing
My pupils are dilating
Goodness, my mouth is so dry

I agree with him that he should come
And check out the rad in my bedroom
Whilst his mate works downstairs

Well, sister don't knock the Gas Man
He knows his stuff
How to give a good service –
You know what I mean
Mmmmm
Did the Gas Man come today you ask?
Yep, he sure did

Alone With My Bed

Would my room be the same if my bed
wasn't there?
My safe haven of rest
Creature comforts so near
Cosy duvet my nest

My safe haven of rest
Sky TV as my mate
Cosy duvet my nest
Interruptions I hate

Sky TV as my mate
In my solitude zone
Interruptions I hate
Don't try to get me on the phone

In my solitude zone
Creature comforts so near
Don't try to get me on the phone
Would my room be the same if my bed
wasn't there?

Your Phone Call

Your phone call
Just one of many on your to do list
Came through unexpected
Catching me off guard
Cutting through my smooth running day

You uttered chilling words in your last call
Which held me at gunpoint
Robbing me of sleep and appetite
Only a barely functioning shell
Left for me to survive with
You pretend to be unaware
Of the damage
Already caused

Today, you speak matter of factly
Threatening my ability to work
Rendering me powerless
Unable to care for my child
Leaving her vulnerable to harm

Your menacing words
Pushed me violently
Of the cliff of stability
Free falling

Rapidly plummeting
Into the chasm
Of an anxiety disorder
The g-force disfiguring my mind
And perspective

I can't think, I can't breath
I can't stop the tears
Emerging over the brim of my eyes
My body trembling out of control
The composure that had accompanied me
Five minutes ago
Has evaporated into thin air
What shall I do?
What can I do?
I can't do anything
Think! Think!
I can't
I'm totally paralysed
By anxiety

Bittersweet

Rich tasty chocolate
Full of promise
You offer continuous orgasmic elation
Without the complications and
Disappointments that come with
A relationship with a man

Always available, melting on my tongue
Exquisite sensations
Anytime, any place, anywhere
You're never too tired, too stressed
You never prefer to go out with your friends
Instead of being with me
You never fail to leave me
Relaxed and fully satisfied

Ah, but there's a sting
No warning of your sneaking
Ability to add to my curves
Causing my clothes to struggle
To cover my body
Buttons straining against buttonholes
Zips unable to make their journey
Giving up, on their task of fastening
A smooth silhouette figure

Transformed to bumpy jelly like bulges
You my dear chocolate
Are no better than him
You both have the power
To take away my self esteem
Enjoyment of life
Leaving me alone
To deal with the aftermath

Brown Stallion

My Brown Stallion
Standing proud
His glistening coat
Pulled taught
Against muscle
He trots around
Eager to be free
His canter escalating to a gallop
Unrestrained

Emancipation
Is marked by velocity
Distance over time
Whooshing winds
Surf along his body
The trees and meadows
Reduced to a green blur
Streaked by hues of browns and blues

As he gallops faster and faster
His strides propel his body to its limits
Bursting joyfully at the opportunity of
Absolute and ultimate control
He bathes himself in ecstasy

On my stallion
The rapid decline from
Thrill to soporific state
Tells me you're finished
Ready to be led back to your stable
Leaving me dreaming of the next time

Love is Not Enough

Sitting here slurping a cup of steaming tea
On a flower-filled May Day
Memories skip in my mind
Like Morris men around a maypole
Creating an intricate pattern
Of different times, places and emotions

I crumble, crushed
As the biggest recollection of all
Shockingly shreds the others to streamers
Oh the pain
So much pain
As I face the fact
That my love was not enough
To stop you slipping away
Through suicide

Lady in Waiting

While I wait for you
I choose to honour you through
The words I speak and the things I do
I try to act wisely with you in mind

While I wait for you
I pray your strength in the Lord
Hoping that you will seek the heart of God
I ask the Lord to equip you
To fulfill your purpose
I offer thanksgiving and praise to God for you

While I wait for you
I accept divine teaching on
Your God ordained position and
How I should relate to you

While I wait for you
I consider our ministerial exchange
You becoming my priest and intercessor
Constantly covering and
Surrounding me with prayer
I ponder your ability to lead me effortlessly
Into the Holy of Holies

While I wait for you
I study and gain insight
Into how I can minister comfort
And be a help to you
How I can be a soothing balm
For you to relax and revel in

While I wait for you
I develop in my ability
To hear the Voice of God
So that I can listen to Him
On behalf of us both
I learn to trust myself enough
To act on what I have heard

While I wait for you
I expand my skills in business and enterprise
I establish a good work ethic
I apply myself to do all things well

My beloved Husband
I am a Lady in Waiting for you

My Standard

My standard
Represents who I am and
What I want to be

My standard
Compels me to assess
Your suitability to be my mate
In 60 seconds
I appraise the image you present before me
Your dress, your hair, your nails
They tell me whether
You will make an effort on my behalf
And whether you have any respect for me

My standard
Causes me to examine whether I would have
To train, mould and shape you
To be the partner I need you to be
A good steward, hostess and ambassador
Or whether you will cause me
To hang my head
In shame on a daily basis

My standard
Doesn't allow me to be bullied
Into submission
Neither does it permit me to
Commit to the woman I love deeply
Upon discovering her mental instability

My standard
Steers me away from
Incompatibility and conflict
Protects me from unhappiness,
Depression and destitution
It paves the way for me to be truly loved
Appreciated and fulfilled

Yes, it's true I am a slave to my standard
But don't condemn it
Don't label it as harsh
Because if you meet my standard
You, my wife will represent who I am
And what I want to be

Virtual Reality

As I reflect on my plump reflection
I think about how you're perceiving me
Spying my body, crafting rejection
My size is all your fleeting glances see
You aren't even really noticing me
You just glimpse the legacy of being
Excluded. I eat to conceal my plea
Emotional turmoil, deeply feeling
The only hunger I clasp with meaning
Is for someone to take the time to know
Me. Find out what I like, stop me kneeling
I'm praying for the chance to let ME show
A visit, a text, an email, a call
To make new friends, is what I want, that's all

Freedom

My daughter
Child of a one night stand
I hope you are happy
With your new family

We never bonded
When you were a baby
You made such a racket
Always miserable
You never understood
That you have to fit into
My lifestyle
Not me into yours

When I met your step-dad
He made me feel great
About myself
We had so much fun
He became the centre of my world
I loved him so much
I knew what he was doing in your bedroom
Even though it was wrong
I tried my best to ignore it
Hoping he'd get bored
And stop one day

But you had to spoil everything
Didn't you
Why couldn't you just bear it?
Until he stopped
He loves us
If you didn't tell your teacher
We would still be
Together as a couple
Now we're separated

You know what?
From the day you were born
You've been more trouble
Than it's worth
I'm glad you're not
My responsibility anymore
Even though I'm in jail
I'm finally free

The Lying Mirror

Mirror, mirror
You once was my faithful friend
Telling me I looked fabulous
Highlighting my curvaceous figure
Informing me that I'd be pleasing to any eye
You kindly and gently showed minor flaws
A few spots or eyebrows out of place

Now you scream vicious lies,
Reflections of once pert breasts drooping
Dimples on my thighs, not my cheeks
You refuse to show me the defining curve
Between my bum and the tops of my legs
Oh and those batwings
So not me

You must be deceiving me
Because the changes are so sudden
The blossoming body of youth
Transformed to this unfamiliar
Middle aged mass
With no signs of any in between stages

I hate you
I don't need you Mirror
I can go for weeks ignoring your presence
Who needs you anyway?

Forgive me old friend
I find it so hard to accept your truth
That I have lost control of my image

A Connection

As your rejection
Slaps me in the face
I reel from the shock
That we didn't share the same feelings
Your truth is that you were
Simply extending a hand of friendship
I saw that hand as one which offered to
Lift me out of my faecal sludge of singleness
Holding my future
Shared home, lives and children
I believe in love at first sight
I thought we had a connection
Nausea overwhelms me as I replay
Our conversation over and over
I don't know what to do
Why have I got it wrong again?

Why I Worship

I worship you
Not because
You have cleansed me
With the blood of your Son
Christ Jesus
Renewing my mind and life

I worship you
Not because
You have given me your Holy Spirit
To journey with me through life
My constant 24/7 partner

I worship you
Not because
Of the many promises
You have made
And fulfilled in my life

I worship you
Not because
Of the daily portions
Of mercy and grace
You have imparted to me

I worship you
Not because
You have given me your Word
To direct me through the route of living

I worship you
Not because
You have given me a peace
That no one can offer

I worship you
Not because
You have carried and supported me through
Difficult circumstances

I worship you
Not because
Someone else told me to

I worship you
Not because
You have granted
Things I've prayed for
Beautiful children
A job, a home
And a whole lot more

I worship you
Not because
You have healed me
In times of sickness and brokenness

Although, all of the above
Are reason enough in themselves for
Worshipping you
Jehovah God
And I thank you

BUT

I worship you
Because
YOU are
The Almighty, Magnificent
God of Heaven and Earth
Determiner of all things
The Supreme Holy King

I know
Who YOU are
And therefore have
No option but to worship
YOU
For Who
YOU Are

Life

When you said
'Life is like running through
A meadow at sunset'
I was both astounded and amazed
How could one so young
Even begin to define life
After all yours is only 11 years old

But you caused me to wonder
At what point did life for me
Become so complicated
So full of deliberation and restrictions

When I asked 'what do you mean?'
You spoke of freedom
And the ability to pursue your dreams
My feeling of pride were tinged with
Personal disappointment

Independence and choice
That's what I want for you
But I examined myself to see if
I have in any way prevented you
From experiencing that level of liberty
Memories flood back of

Missed opportunities
I have simply allowed to happen
In my own life

So my Son
I will learn from your wise words
Kick of my shoes
Live life to the full
The fact is
It's too short
Not to

Running

What did you hope to gain
From running away?
Your prison is not marked by a
Building with a HMP sign
Neither is it defined by four walls
Circumstances are not the bricks
Of your round the clock incarceration
It has been built by
Selfishness, self-centeredness
Your self absorption means
That you don't ever take others into account
Now you suffer dismissal at every turn
Isolated and alone
You try to escape your desolation

Cheesecake

Love is like a cheesecake
The fruity, sugary topping
Resembling the sweetness
Of falling in love
Delicious sensations
Giddy euphoria
Creating an insatiable
Desire for more

The creamy centre
Melting in your mouth
Each moment to be savoured
Leaving you looking
Forward eagerly to the next
Dating, marriage
Fashioned together
By incredible shared experiences
Driving you to create more

The crumbly biscuit base
Adds texture and variation
Arguments and upset
Make room for reconciliation
The appreciation of differences
Teaching me to forgive more

As I sit here relishing each mouthful
Of this delicious cheesecake
I reflect on the veracity
That love is a mouthful of all layers

Lost

My friend I see the tears
Running down your heart
I hear your silent sobs
Mourning a marriage
That once comprised of
Happy lives entwined as one
Now conversations
Hang in the air like a misty fog
Nothing really tangible
You speak of living a single life
Within your marriage
Leaving you with nothing to hug
But loneliness
Every time you see him
Anger and resentment rise up
Like fiery flames reducing
Any interaction to ashes
So avoidance seems
A brilliant solution
You describe the long
Journey you have made
From kidding yourself
That everything is ok
To a place of bereavement
And acceptance that things have changed

Every day you look in the mirror
The face looking back asks
Why are you remaining this relationship?
How can you free yourself
From the hourly pain?

You seek my advice
I can't tell you what to do
You're the one who has to live
With your choices
What can I say?
Divorce is not the end
It only ends the contract
Not the relationship
The frustrations will continue
Year in year out
It just that you don't have
To live with them 24/7

Seeing You

As I sit on the bus
I spot you
Your interesting lips
The shape of your walnut coloured eyes
Framed by long black lashes
They fill me with exhilaration
I try desperately not to stare
But the compulsion
Transcends potential embarrassment
You sit in your seat oblivious to me
Going about your daily business
As the engine rumbles
Time for me to make a move
Runs like sand through a timer
Words snag in my throat
Unable to escape
Our eyes lock as you get off
Another opportunity
Gets run over by the wheels of a bus

Yesterday

When you told me today
That you have just
Discovered yesterday
I was speechless
Not quite knowing what to say
Whichever way you cut it
You can only discover yesterday today

When you announced that you will spend
Tomorrow and the following day
Focusing on yesterday
I thought of the lives
Half lived, wasted, immobilised
By doing just that
Such a travesty

You and I both know that
You had discovered
A TV channel new to you
But you left me thinking of those
Who live in the shadows
To scared to face a vibrant future today

Tuesday – Sunday, 11am – 8pm
T +44 (0)20 7921 0943
F +44 (0)20 7921 0607
poetrylibrary.org.uk

Level 5 at Royal Festival Hall
Southbank Centre, Belvedere R

POETRY L

The Saison Poetry
the Arts Council Po